Little
Big Giant

Stories of Wisdom and Inspiration

Nnedi Okorafor

Award-Winning Author of Speculative Fiction

Copyright © 2024 Little Big Giant

No part of this publication may be reproduced, stored in a retrieval system, or transmitted in any form or by any means, electronic, mechanical, photocopying, recording, or otherwise, without the prior written permission of the publisher.

Printed in the United States of America

First Edition: 2024

This copyright page includes the necessary copyright notice, permissions request information, acknowledgments for the cover design, interior design, and editing, as well as the details of the first edition.

www.littlebiggiant.com

Disclaimer: This book is a work of non-fiction and is intended for informational and educational purposes only. The names in this biography are trademarks of their respective owners. This book is not affiliated with, endorsed by, or sponsored by any of these trademark holders. The use of these names is intended solely to provide context and historical reference.

The author makes no claims to ownership of any trademarks or copyrights associated with the names and likenesses of the individuals referenced in this book. Any opinions expressed in this book are those of the author and do not reflect the views of any wrestling promotion or trademark holder.

Introduction

Nnedi Okorafor, a celebrated author of speculative fiction, was born in the vibrant city of Chicago to Nigerian immigrant parents. From a young age, she was captivated by the stories of her heritage, weaving them into her imagination. At just 19, a life-altering event changed everything: a rare medical condition left her paralyzed for a time, but instead of succumbing to despair, she transformed her experience into a powerful source of inspiration. This resilience fueled her creativity, leading to the creation of worlds where magic and technology intertwine, and where African culture takes center stage. With multiple awards under her belt, including the Hugo and Nebula, her journey is a testament to the power of storytelling. But what secrets lie behind her extraordinary tales? The answers may just be as fantastical as the worlds she creates.

Table of Contents

Table of Contents..6
Chapter 1... 9
Early Life and Cultural Influences........................ 9
Chapter 2... 16
Discovering Writing.. 16
Chapter 3... 23
Overcoming Obstacles.......................................23
Chapter 4... 30
African Futurism...30
Chapter 5... 40
Awards and Recognition.................................... 40
Chapter 6... 47
Writing Process and Inspiration......................... 47
Chapter 7... 58
Diversity in Literature... 58
Chapter 8... 66
Environmental Activism......................................66

Chapter 9.. **75**
Adapting Work to Other Mediums........................... 75
Chapter 10.. **83**
Legacy and Future Plans.. 83

Chapter 1

Early Life and Cultural Influences

Once upon a time, in the vibrant heart of Nigeria, a little girl named Nnedi Okorafor was born. Picture a bustling town filled with colorful markets, the sounds of laughter, and the aroma of spicy jollof rice wafting through the air. Nnedi grew up in a family that was as lively as the streets around them. Her parents, both Nigerian immigrants, settled in the city of Aba, where the sun shone brightly, and the sky was a dazzling blue.

From a young age, Nnedi was surrounded by stories. Not just any stories, but tales steeped in the rich tapestry of African mythology. Imagine sitting around a fire at night, the stars twinkling above, as her grandmother spun yarns about the legendary trickster spider, Anansi, or the mighty warrior, Shaka Zulu. These stories weren't just entertainment; they were lessons wrapped in excitement, teaching Nnedi about bravery, cunning, and the importance of community. She learned that every character had a purpose, and every tale had a lesson, shaping her understanding of the world.

But it wasn't just the myths that influenced Nnedi. Her family played a huge role in her life, too. Her father was a professor, always encouraging her to ask questions and think critically. "Why does the sky turn orange at sunset?" he'd say, with a twinkle in his eye. Her mother, a caring nurse, taught her the value of compassion and hard work. Nnedi often helped her mom at the hospital, witnessing the impact of kindness and dedication firsthand. The warmth of her family made her feel safe, allowing her imagination to run wild.

The community around her was a treasure trove of culture. Nnedi spent afternoons playing with her friends, creating games inspired by the stories they heard. They'd pretend to be brave heroes, embarking on epic quests to save the day. And, oh boy, did they get into some silly adventures! Like the time they decided to build a "spaceship" out of cardboard boxes and ended up tumbling down a hill, laughing uncontrollably. These moments were filled with joy, teaching Nnedi the importance of friendship and collaboration.

As she grew older, Nnedi began to realize how these experiences shaped her. The blend of her rich Nigerian heritage, the lessons from her family, and the fun of her community all ignited a spark in her imagination. She felt a strong connection to her roots, and it became clear that these influences would fuel her future stories. Nnedi started to write, weaving together the magic of her childhood with the wisdom of her ancestors.

So, as you can see, Nnedi Okorafor's early life was like a colorful tapestry, woven with threads of culture, family, and adventure. Each piece was essential in shaping her into the remarkable storyteller she would become. The laughter, the myths, and the love of her community created a foundation that would support her dreams.

Key Takeaway: Our early experiences and the people around us shape who we are. Embrace your culture, learn from your family, and let your imagination run wild! You never know how it might inspire your own stories.

Chapter 2

Discovering Writing

Nnedi Okorafor had a love for books that was as big as the sky over Nigeria. Like, imagine a kid who could spend hours in a library, surrounded by stories that made her heart race and her imagination soar! From a young age, she was captivated by tales of magical creatures, brave heroes, and far-off lands. She would often sneak into her family's living room, where her mom would read to her and her siblings. The way her mom brought stories to life was like watching a magician perform tricks! Nnedi knew that one day, she wanted to create her own magic with words.

Now, let's talk about Nnedi's first writing experience, which was a bit of a wild ride. One day, she was in school, and her teacher announced a writing competition. Nnedi was super excited but also kind of nervous. She had never written anything for a contest before! With a deep breath, she decided to write a story about a girl who could talk to animals. The moment she put pen to paper, it was like a door to another world swung open. She could see the animals, hear their voices, and feel the girl's adventures. When she finished, she couldn't believe how much fun it was! Nnedi didn't win the competition, but she learned something way more important: writing made her feel alive!

After that, Nnedi was on a mission. She started writing everything she could think of—short stories, poems, and even little comic strips! She knew she wanted to pursue writing as a career, but that wasn't always easy. Nnedi faced some tough choices along the way. People would sometimes tell her that writing was just a hobby and that she should focus on something "more practical." But Nnedi was like, "No way! I'm going to be a writer!" With each story she wrote, her confidence grew, and she started to believe that her voice mattered.

She also realized that her unique perspective, influenced by her Nigerian roots and love for African mythology, could bring something special to the world of literature. It was like she had a treasure chest of stories waiting to be shared! So, she set off on a journey to find her place in the literary world. She read everything she could get her hands on, attended writing workshops, and even joined online communities where she could connect with other writers.

Nnedi's determination paid off. She eventually got her first book published, and it was like fireworks going off in her heart! She was finally living her dream. But the adventure didn't stop there. Nnedi knew she wanted to write stories that inspired kids like her, stories that were filled with magic, adventure, and a sprinkle of humor. She wanted to show young readers that they could be heroes in their own stories, just like the characters she loved.

And so, with a notebook in one hand and a dream in the other, Nnedi Okorafor embarked on her writing journey. She learned that storytelling wasn't just about words on a page; it was about connecting with others, sharing experiences, and sparking imaginations.

Key Takeaway: Writing is a powerful way to express yourself and share your unique stories with the world. Don't be afraid to follow your passion, even if others doubt you. Your voice matters!

Chapter 3

Overcoming Obstacles

Nnedi Okorafor's journey wasn't all sunshine and rainbows, like, at all. Imagine a superhero trying to save the day but facing some seriously tough challenges. That was Nnedi. One of her biggest battles was with scoliosis—a condition that made her spine curve like a question mark. Can you picture that? Instead of standing tall and straight, Nnedi had to deal with pain and discomfort. But guess what? She didn't let it define her. Instead, she learned to embrace her uniqueness, like a superhero flaunting a cool cape.

Every time Nnedi walked into a room, she was like, "Yeah, I've got scoliosis, but that's just part of my story!" She became super creative, using her experiences to inspire her characters and stories. When she wrote about strong, resilient heroines who faced their own challenges, she was, in a way, writing about herself. Her stories became a canvas for all the struggles she had to overcome, and they painted a picture of hope and courage.

But that wasn't the only hurdle Nnedi had to jump over. Oh no! She also faced rejection. Yup, even the most talented writers get told "no" sometimes. Imagine sending out a story you poured your heart into, only to have it come back with a big fat "not for us." Ouch! That's gotta hurt, right? But instead of giving up and throwing her laptop out the window (which, let's be honest, would be a little dramatic), Nnedi picked herself up, dusted off her keyboard, and tried again.

She learned that rejection was just a stepping stone, not a dead end. It was like a puzzle she had to solve, and she was determined to find the missing piece. Each "no" made her more determined to succeed. Nnedi kept writing, kept submitting, and kept believing in herself. She became a master at turning setbacks into comebacks, and that's a lesson we can all learn from.

And you know what? It was her perseverance and resilience that really set her apart. Picture a bamboo tree: it bends but doesn't break. Nnedi was like that bamboo tree. When life threw challenges at her, she didn't just bend; she grew stronger. She used her struggles to fuel her passion for storytelling. Instead of letting obstacles stop her, she turned them into fuel for her creativity.

Nnedi's journey reminds us that obstacles can be turned into opportunities. She taught us that it's okay to stumble as long as you get back up and keep going.

Her ability to face challenges head-on and keep pushing forward is something we can all admire.

So, what's the key takeaway from Nnedi's story? Well, kids, it's simple: No matter how tough things get, never give up on your dreams. Obstacles are just part of the adventure, and with a little perseverance and a lot of heart, you can overcome anything. Just like Nnedi, you have the power to turn your struggles into something amazing!

And remember, every time you face a challenge, think of it as a chance to grow stronger and write your own epic story.

Chapter 4

African Futurism

Have you ever imagined a world where ancient myths blend with futuristic technology? Well, welcome to the realm of African Futurism! This vibrant and exciting genre is like a cosmic bridge connecting Africa's rich cultural heritage with the limitless possibilities of the future. Picture this: towering skyscrapers made of shimmering, colorful materials, and flying cars zipping through the skies, all while the spirits of ancestors watch over the land. Sounds cool, right?

African Futurism is not just about flashy gadgets and wild adventures; it's a celebration of African culture, stories, and identity. Writers like Nnedi Okorafor have become pioneers in this genre, creating tales that incorporate African mythology, folklore, and traditions into the fabric of science fiction. Imagine a superhero with the power of a trickster god, or a brave heroine who communicates with the spirits of her ancestors to solve mysteries! These stories remind us that our history and culture are not just relics of the past but living, breathing elements that shape our future.

So, how does this all work? Well, let's take a closer look. When Nnedi Okorafor writes, she weaves in the vibrant threads of her Nigerian roots. Her characters often face challenges that reflect real-world issues, like climate change or the importance of community. For instance, in her novel "Binti," the protagonist is a young Himba woman who uses her cultural practices to navigate a galaxy filled with different species and technology. It's like she's saying, "Hey, your background is not just a part of you; it's a superpower!"

And that's where the magic happens! By incorporating cultural elements into science fiction, Okorafor and other African Futurists are breaking barriers in a genre that has often sidelined diverse voices. They're not just telling stories; they're reshaping the narrative landscape. They challenge the notion that futuristic tales can only be told through a Western lens. Instead, they show that the future can be bright and beautiful, filled with characters who look like us and come from backgrounds that reflect the richness of our world.

But wait, there's more! African Futurism is also about humor and heart. Think of it as a rollercoaster ride where you're laughing one moment and holding your breath the next. Characters often find themselves in silly situations—like trying to outsmart a mischievous spirit or getting caught in a hilarious misunderstanding with aliens. These moments remind us that while the future may be unknown, laughter is a universal language that connects us all.

Now, let's not forget about the mysteries! Many African Futurist stories are packed with puzzles that keep readers on the edge of their seats. Imagine trying to decode a message from an ancient artifact that holds the key to saving a planet! It's like being a detective in a sci-fi world where every clue matters. This sense of urgency and excitement pulls readers in, making them feel like they're part of the adventure.

As we dive deeper into African Futurism, it's clear that it's not just a genre; it's a movement. Writers are using their voices to advocate for representation, showing young readers that they, too, can dream big and create their own futures. By embracing their cultures and experiences, they inspire a new generation of storytellers who will continue to break barriers and explore new frontiers.

So, what can we take away from this thrilling journey into African Futurism?

Well, it's simple: Your culture is a treasure chest of stories waiting to be told. Whether you're writing, drawing, or dreaming, remember that your unique background can shape the future in ways you never imagined. Embrace your heritage, celebrate your identity, and let your imagination soar!

Key Takeaway

Your culture is a powerful tool that can help you tell amazing stories. Embrace it, and who knows what incredible adventures you might create!

Chapter 5

Awards and Recognition

Nnedi Okorafor is not just a storyteller; she's a superhero in the literary world! And just like any superhero, she's received some shiny awards that recognize her incredible talents. You might have heard of the Hugo and Nebula

Awards—these are like the Oscars of science fiction and fantasy writing. Winning these awards is a big deal, and Nnedi snagged both!

The Hugo Award, named after Hugo Gernsback, who was a pioneer in science fiction publishing, is given annually to the best works in the genre. Nnedi won this prestigious award for her novel *Binti*, which is about a young woman from the Himba tribe who travels to a prestigious intergalactic university. Imagine that! A girl from a small village in Namibia going off to space! It's like the ultimate adventure, and it shows how her stories connect African culture with futuristic ideas.

Then there's the Nebula Award, which is awarded by the Science Fiction and Fantasy Writers of America. Nnedi received this honor for the same book, *Binti*. Winning these awards not only put her on the map but also highlighted the importance of African voices in science fiction. It was like a signal flare in the sky, saying, "Hey, the future can be bright and diverse!"

But wait, there's more! Nnedi's not just a one-hit-wonder. She has received a treasure chest of other accolades, too. From the World Fantasy Award to the Locus Award, her shelves must be bursting with trophies! These awards celebrate her unique style and the way she weaves African mythology into her stories, making them both relatable and fantastical.

Did you know that her work has sparked conversations about diversity in literature? Nnedi's stories are not just entertaining; they challenge the norms of the literary world. By showcasing characters from various backgrounds, she inspires young readers to dream big and believe that their stories matter, too. She's like a literary magician, pulling diverse characters and stories out of her hat!

Her impact on the literary world is immense. Nnedi is opening doors for new voices and paving the way for future generations of writers. She's showing that anyone can be a hero in their own story, no matter where they come from. When kids read her books, they not only get to go on thrilling adventures but also learn about their own cultures and histories.

In interviews, Nnedi often talks about how she wants her stories to be a bridge—connecting people from different backgrounds and experiences. This is what makes her work so special. It's not just about the awards; it's about the conversations her books inspire.

So, the next time you hear about Nnedi Okorafor winning another award, remember that it's not just a trophy on a shelf. It's a celebration of diversity, imagination, and the power of storytelling.

Nnedi's journey is a reminder that your voice matters and that stories can change the world!

Key Takeaway: Awards are great, but the real treasure lies in the stories we tell and the connections we make. Everyone has a story worth sharing!

Chapter 6

Writing Process and Inspiration

Nnedi Okorafor sat at her desk, the sunlight streaming through her window, illuminating a colorful array of sticky notes, notebooks, and her trusty laptop. This was her creative fortress, where ideas danced like fireflies and stories took flight. But where did all that inspiration come from? Well, buckle up, because Nnedi's writing process is as vibrant and lively as her tales!

Sources of Inspiration

Nnedi often said that inspiration was like a treasure map—sometimes it led you to hidden gems, and other times it took you on wild adventures! One of her favorite sources of inspiration was the rich tapestry of African mythology. She would dive into the stories of ancient gods and heroes, letting their epic tales swirl around in her mind. Did you know that in some African cultures, stories are considered a way to pass down wisdom and history? Nnedi took that wisdom and wove it into her own stories, creating characters that felt as real as the friends she met in her childhood.

But it wasn't just myths that sparked her imagination. Nnedi loved to observe the world around her. Whether it was the bustling streets of Lagos or the serene beauty of nature, she found stories everywhere! She believed that every person she met had a tale to tell. This curiosity about the world helped her create characters that were relatable and full of life. For instance, the idea for her novel "Who Fears Death" came from a mix of her own experiences and the historical struggles of her ancestors. Talk about inspiration!

Writing Rituals and Habits

Now, let's talk about how Nnedi turned those sparks of inspiration into actual stories. She had some pretty quirky writing rituals that made the process fun! Every morning, she would brew a cup of her favorite tea—peppermint, if you're curious—and light a candle. The warm, cozy aroma helped her focus and set the mood for creativity. It was like her own little magic potion!

Nnedi also believed in the power of music. She would create playlists that matched the tone of her stories. If she was writing a thrilling adventure, you could bet there were some upbeat tunes blasting through her speakers. And when it was time to write a more emotional scene, she'd switch to soft, haunting melodies. This helped her get into the right headspace and brought her characters to life in ways that made readers feel every emotion.

But, like many kids juggling school and hobbies, Nnedi had to balance her writing with her teaching. Yep, she was a professor, which meant she had to inspire the next generation of writers while also working on her own stories. She often joked that her classroom was like a mini-writers' workshop, where students shared their ideas and helped each other grow. She loved hearing their stories and often used their creativity as fuel for her own writing. It was a win-win situation!

Balancing Writing and Teaching

Imagine trying to write an epic novel while also grading papers and preparing lectures! Nnedi had to master the art of time management. She created a schedule that allowed her to dedicate time to both her students and her writing. This meant setting aside specific hours for writing, just like a superhero sets aside time to save the day. She would often say, "If you want to be a writer, you have to write—just like if you want to be a superhero, you have to practice your powers!"

Nnedi also found that teaching made her a better writer. Explaining complex ideas to her students helped her clarify her own thoughts and push her creative boundaries. And, of course, her students kept her young at heart with their wild ideas and boundless energy. It was like having a front-row seat to a never-ending show of creativity!

So, whether she was sipping tea at her desk, jamming to her favorite tunes, or engaging with her students, Nnedi's writing process was a delightful blend of inspiration, ritual, and balance. She taught us that creativity doesn't just come from solitude; it can thrive in community and connection.

Key Takeaway

Every writer has their own unique process, and finding what inspires you is the first step to creating amazing stories.

Embrace your surroundings, connect with others, and don't be afraid to develop your own rituals. Who knows? You might just discover the next great adventure waiting to be written!

Chapter 7

Diversity in Literature

Have you ever noticed how some books feel like they take you on a wild ride through different worlds? Well, that's the magic of diversity in literature! Imagine diving into stories that don't just mirror one way of life but open the door to a universe filled with colors, cultures, and experiences. This chapter is all about why that's super important, especially for young readers like you.

First off, let's talk about the importance of diversity in literature. Books that feature a variety of characters and cultures help us understand that the world is a big, beautiful place. It's like adding sprinkles to ice cream—each sprinkle represents a different flavor and together they make the treat way more exciting! When kids read about characters from different backgrounds, they learn to appreciate the differences and similarities among people. It's a bit like a treasure map that leads to empathy and understanding, showing that everyone has a story worth telling.

Now, if we want more of these amazing stories, we have to advocate for representation. This means that we need to speak up and encourage writers, publishers, and schools to include more diverse voices in literature. Imagine if all the superheroes in comic books were the same—boring, right? We need heroes of all shapes, sizes, and backgrounds to inspire us! Nnedi Okorafor, for example, uses her Nigerian heritage to create characters that reflect her culture. By championing diverse authors and stories, we not only get to enjoy richer narratives but also help young readers see themselves in the pages. It's like holding a mirror up to the world and saying, "Look! You matter!"

But what's the impact on young readers? Well, studies show that when kids read diverse books, they develop a better understanding of others and themselves. Think of it as training wheels for compassion! When you read about someone who looks or lives differently from you, it can spark curiosity and open up conversations about culture, identity, and even friendship. Plus, diverse stories can help kids feel less alone. If a character faces challenges similar to yours, it's like having a buddy who gets you, even if they're from a different part of the world.

Diversity in literature also encourages creativity. When you see a wide range of characters and stories, it inspires you to think outside the box and come up with your own unique tales. Who knows? Maybe one day, you'll write a story that helps another kid feel understood or inspired!

As we wrap up this chapter, remember that advocating for diversity in literature is a team effort. Whether you're sharing a book recommendation with friends or encouraging your teachers to include diverse authors in the curriculum, every little action counts.

Key Takeaway: Reading diverse literature not only broadens your perspective but also helps you understand

and connect with people from different backgrounds. So, dive into a variety of stories and let your imagination soar!

Chapter 8

Environmental Activism

Nnedi Okorafor always felt a special connection to nature. Growing up in Nigeria, she spent countless afternoons wandering through lush green forests, feeling the cool breeze on her skin and listening to the vibrant sounds of wildlife. It was like the trees whispered secrets, and the rivers sang songs only she could hear. This deep bond with the environment shaped her worldview, making her acutely aware of the pressing environmental issues facing our planet.

Did you know that Africa is home to some of the most diverse ecosystems in the world? From the Sahara Desert to the rainforests of the Congo, each region has its unique plants and animals. Unfortunately, these beautiful habitats are under threat from climate change, pollution, and deforestation. Nnedi's love for nature pushed her to not just observe these issues but to actively engage with them. She realized that her writing could be a powerful tool for activism, shining a light on the urgent need to protect the environment.

In her stories, Nnedi weaves in themes of environmentalism, showcasing how interconnected we all are with nature. For instance, in her novel "Binti," she explores the relationship between humanity and the environment through the lens of a young woman who travels across galaxies. She highlights the importance of preserving cultures and ecosystems, reminding readers that every action we take has consequences. It's like a ripple effect—throw a stone into a pond, and the ripples spread far and wide. Nnedi's characters often find themselves facing challenges that require them to think about their impact on the world around them, encouraging young readers to consider their own choices.

But wait, there's more! Nnedi's activism doesn't stop at her writing. She's actively involved in initiatives that promote environmental awareness. She participates in discussions, panels, and events that focus on sustainability and the importance of preserving our planet. By sharing her knowledge and passion, she inspires others to take action. She believes that everyone, no matter how small, can make a difference. It's like that saying, "Be the change you wish to see in the world." Nnedi embodies this idea, showing that even writers can be warriors for the environment.

In one of her humorous anecdotes, she once recounted a time when she tried to plant a garden in her backyard. Let's just say it didn't go as planned. Instead of a flourishing vegetable patch, she ended up with a collection of very confused squirrels and a few stubborn weeds. But instead of feeling defeated, she laughed it off, saying, "At least the squirrels are well-fed!" This lighthearted moment reminds us that activism doesn't have to be serious all the time. Sometimes, it's about finding joy in the journey, even when things don't go as expected.

Through her stories and actions, Nnedi Okorafor has made a significant impact on environmental awareness. She encourages her readers to think critically about the world around them and to recognize the importance of protecting our planet. By blending her love for storytelling with her passion for nature, she shows that literature can be a powerful force for change.

So, what can you take away from this chapter? Here's the key takeaway: You have the power to make a difference! Whether it's through writing, speaking up, or simply being mindful of your choices, every little action counts in protecting our environment. So, go ahead and be a superhero for the planet!

Chapter 9

Adapting Work to Other Mediums

Have you ever read a book and thought, "Wow, this would make an awesome comic!"? Well, Nnedi Okorafor took that idea and ran with it! She's not just a writer of novels; she's a master at transforming her stories into graphic novels. It's like taking a delicious cake and turning it into cupcakes—each one is a little different but just as tasty!

One of her most popular novels, *Akata Witch*, was adapted into a graphic novel, and let me tell you, it was a hit! The vibrant illustrations brought the characters to life in a whole new way. You could almost feel the magic jumping off the pages! Nnedi worked closely with talented artists to ensure that the spirit of her story was captured perfectly. Imagine how exciting it must be for kids to see their favorite characters in full color, leaping off the page with their adventures!

And speaking of adventures, Nnedi didn't stop there. She teamed up with none other than Marvel Comics! Yup, you heard that right. Marvel, the home of superheroes like Spider-Man and Iron Man, recognized Nnedi's incredible talent. They collaborated on a series called *Black Panther: Long Live the King*, which featured the famous Wakandan hero. Nnedi infused her unique style and cultural richness into the story, making it a thrilling blend of superhero action and African mythology. Just picture it: a fierce battle in Wakanda, with Nnedi's words dancing alongside the stunning artwork. It's like a superhero movie unfolding right before your eyes!

But wait, there's more! Nnedi is also bringing her stories to the screen. Yep, that's right! She's working on adapting her novels into TV shows and films. Imagine sitting down to watch a series that takes you on a wild ride through the worlds she's created, filled with magic, adventure, and characters that feel like friends. It's like having your own personal portal to another universe! The excitement of seeing her characters and stories come to life in a different format is something that keeps fans on the edge of their seats.

Nnedi's ability to adapt her work shows how stories can transcend mediums, reaching new audiences and sparking imaginations everywhere. Whether it's through the pages of a graphic novel, the action-packed frames of a comic, or the moving images of a screen, her stories remind us that creativity knows no bounds.

So, what can we learn from Nnedi Okorafor's journey in adapting her work? Well, it's all about being flexible and open to new ideas. Just like Nnedi, you can take your own stories and explore different ways to share them with the world. Who knows? Maybe you'll create the next big thing in storytelling!

Key Takeaway: Creativity has no limits! Don't be afraid to explore different ways to tell your stories, whether through writing, art, or even film. Your imagination can take you anywhere!

Chapter 10

Legacy and Future Plans

Nnedi Okorafor has become a beacon of light for young readers and aspiring writers around the world. Imagine a kid sitting in their room, surrounded by stacks of books, with a spark of creativity bubbling inside them. That's the kind of magic Nnedi brings to the table! She's not just an author; she's a mentor, a guide, and a source of inspiration. Her stories resonate with young minds, urging them to explore their own imaginations and embrace their unique identities.

    Her impact on young readers is like a ripple in a pond—spreading far and wide. Kids see characters that look like them, live in worlds they can relate to, and face challenges that mirror their own. Nnedi's characters are often strong, courageous, and deeply connected to their roots, showing young readers that their backgrounds can fuel their creativity. When kids read her books, they're not just entertained; they're learning about resilience, diversity, and the importance of believing in themselves.

But wait, there's more! Nnedi isn't stopping anytime soon. She's got big plans for the future, and they're as exciting as a roller coaster ride! One of her goals is to continue writing stories that push boundaries and break stereotypes. She dreams of crafting more tales that blend science fiction with African culture, giving young readers a taste of worlds they've never imagined. And guess what? She's also working on new projects that explore themes of technology and its impact on society. How cool is that?

Nnedi's future projects are like treasure chests waiting to be opened, filled with stories that will thrill and inspire. She's even exploring collaborations with other artists and writers, creating a community of creativity that encourages everyone to share their voices. Imagine a world where kids can read stories that reflect their experiences and ignite their imaginations!

But Nnedi's mission doesn't stop with her own writing. She's all about lifting others up and inspiring the next generation of storytellers. She believes that everyone has a story to tell, and she's committed to breaking barriers for underrepresented voices in literature. Nnedi's work encourages kids to express themselves and to realize that their stories matter. She's paving the way for future authors to step into the spotlight, reminding them that their backgrounds and experiences are valuable assets in the world of storytelling.

In a world that sometimes feels divided, Nnedi's legacy is a powerful reminder of the importance of unity and representation. Her stories are a bridge that connects cultures and fosters understanding. Kids reading her work can see the beauty in diversity and the strength that comes from embracing who they are.

As Nnedi continues her journey, she's not just writing for today; she's writing for the future. She's planting seeds of creativity and empowerment in the hearts of young readers everywhere. And who knows? Maybe one of those kids will grow up to be the next great author, inspired by Nnedi's incredible journey!

Key Takeaway: Your background and experiences are powerful tools for storytelling. Embrace them, and don't be afraid to share your unique voice with the world!

Dear Reader,

Thank you for choosing "Little Big Giant - Stories of Wisdom and Inspiration"! We hope this book has inspired and motivated you on your own journey to success.

If you enjoyed reading this book and believe in the power of its message, we kindly ask for your support. Please consider leaving a positive review on the platform where you purchased the book. Your review will help spread the message to more young readers, empowering them to dream big and achieve greatness. We acknowledge that mistakes can happen, and we appreciate your forgiveness.

Remember, the overall message of this book is the key. Thank you for being a part of our mission to inspire and uplift young minds.

Printed in Great Britain
by Amazon